The Book of Aberystwyth

Six poets on the art of Clive Hicks-Jenkins

To Carolyn,
with love from
Mary & Adrian

The Book of Ystwyth
Six poets on the art of Clive Hicks-Jenkins

Dave Bonta
Callum James
Andrea Selch
Catriona Urquhart
Damian Walford Davies
Marly Youmans

Carolina Wren Press
Grey Mare Press

First published in 2011 by

Carolina Wren Press

and Grey Mare Press in association with

Llyfrgell Genedlaethol Cymru
The National Library of Wales

Carolina Wren Press
120 Morris Street
Durham
North Carolina 27701
USA
+1* 919-560-2738
carolinawrenpress.org

Grey Mare Press
+44 (0) 560 260 7405
www.greymarepress.co.uk

Library of Congress Cataloging-in-Publication Data
The book of Ystwyth : six poets on the art of Clive
Hicks-Jenkins / by Dave Bonta ... [et al.].
p. cm.
ISBN 978-0-932112-89-7 (alk. paper)
1. Hicks-Jenkins, Clive—Poetry.
2. American poetry—21st century.
3. English poetry—21st century.
I. Bonta, Dave, 1966–
PS617.B66 2011   821'.9208—dc22   2011012273

Edited by Peter Wakelin
Printed in Wales by Gomer Press Ltd

Acknowledgements:
'Green George' was first published in Damian Walford
Davies, *Suit of Lights* (Seren, Bridgend, 2009). The three
poems by Catriona Urquhart were first published in
Catriona Urquhart and Clive Hicks-Jenkins, *The Mare's
Tale* (The Old Stile Press, Llandogo, 2001) and are
included by permission of Ian Hamilton.

Contents

Introduction

Clive Hicks-Jenkins' vast, dark drawing *Tend* shows an old man in pyjamas being shaved by a naked youth. When it was first exhibited many people were affected by recognising the old man as the artist's father in his final illness. Later, the picture was displayed in the Nazi prison barracks at the Terezín holocaust memorial near Prague. Viewers there were moved to tears after their hours visiting the yards and cells, reading in the image not Clive's father but a frail elder in the striped uniform of the concentration camps, tenderly cared for through the grace and life-force of a younger inmate.

In these circumstances, the drawing's power proved to lie not in its specifics but in its expression of universal disparities: age and youth, fear and fortitude, pride and vulnerability, humanity and inhumanity. In Terezín's echoing spaces, a work quarried from the artist's personal experience was capable of finding other meaning.

Narratives and images affect and enrich one another, which is probably why theatre evolved from storytelling, and why children's books are illustrated. The tradition of ekphrasis (making visual art inspired by literature or literature prompted by art) has created memorable reflections, from the shock of Dürer's engravings from The Book of Revelation to the quietude of Auden's discovery in Bruegel of 'how everything turns away / Quite leisurely from the disaster'.

One of the poets in this book, Damian Walford Davies, has written about the ekphrastic power of Clive Hicks-Jenkins' work.* Clive has often been prompted by literature to develop his themes, most potently by Seamus Heaney's poem 'Kevin and the Blackbird', Simon Armitage's translation of *Gawain and the Green Knight*, Peter Shaffer's play *Equus* and stories from the Bible. In turn, his art, in just a few years, has seen a remarkable engagement by poets who have felt driven to respond to it. Six of those poets are represented in this anthology.†

The connections between the poets' words and Clive's images have come about in several different ways. In the late 1990s, Clive and his friend Catriona Urquhart knocked a ball of ideas back and forth between them, creating poems and new images in sequence and finally producing a book together with The Old Stile Press. More recently, Marly Youmans, Damian Walford Davies, Andrea Selch and Dave Bonta have been moved to respond to paintings, and the resulting poems have opened new doorways into their subject matter or new windows to prospects beyond. (Marly Youmans and the novelist Kathe Koja have also written prose responses to the paintings, published in the book *Clive Hicks-Jenkins*). Callum James discovered such resounding counterpoint between his existing poems on the Stations of the Cross and Clive's Mari Lwyd drawings that they demanded to be partnered; later he wrote further poems inspired by Clive's paintings about Hervé and the wolf.

Putting some of the poems that have been written by these six poets alongside the paintings in this little book allows each to illuminate the other. Words are abstract; even figurative or narrative paintings may put up barriers to understanding. But words and images together? The partnership of poems and pictures helps the eye to travel further through the imagery, helps bring forth richer thoughts. For the reader-viewer the association may begin a new ekphrastic journey, into his or her own experience and imagination. And undoubtedly, there will be more poems, more paintings, and more responses still to come.

Peter Wakelin

---

* 'Furious Embrace: Clive Hicks-Jenkins among the Poets', in *Clive Hicks-Jenkins* by Simon Callow, Andrew Green, Rex Harley, Clive Hicks-Jenkins, Kathe Koja, Anita Mills, Montserrat Prat, Jacqueline Thalmann, Damian Walford Davies, Marly Youmans (Lund Humphries, London, 2011)
† The original British or American spelling and arrangement is retained in each poem.

Damian Walford Davies

Born in Aberystwyth in 1971, DAMIAN WALFORD DAVIES has taught in the Department of English and Creative Writing at Aberystwyth University since 1997. A co-written collection of poems, *Whiteout*, appeared from Parthian in 2006, and his first full collection, *Suit of Lights*, was published by Seren in 2009. His second Seren collection, *Alabaster Girls*, will appear in 2012. Committed to a poetry of irony and subversive play, his work explores the darker side of the lyric. He has just completed a narrative collection entitled *Witch*, a period-parable that explores the 'making' of a witch in the tense, weird atmosphere of 1640s Suffolk.

Green George

Altar-
piece of spliced time:

the indie
damsel and dog an indi-

fferent audience
for the renegade cowboy-

fusilier with
Tommyhat and quilted

carmine horse
debouching from Oxwich

onto a Gol-
gotha meadow of camp-

anula to
spear a blue-tongued

gummy devil-
dragon and the tide lolls in.

The Writing in the Dust

Under the lush skirt
of the mountain

just the slow camber
of a body feathering

into a bird, plucking
from itself that quill

of an arm, coming so
close to her we could

smell the hung gush
of her hair under

the mule's halter,
her kitten heels

arching their backs
to hiss in our ears,

the stones we held
now brittle as eggs.

Still, life

The black hammock
stirs to siren music
from the curtains' lyre.

The tune says: you are
stranded, little dogfish,
unborn in your purse;

you will dry; your mottled
mother with cats' eyes
bays for you beyond

the table's strandline:
hail her, little nursehound,
with those frantic cords,

scrawl your panic on that
strip of darkening sea.
Behind you are the tear-

drop shells they snared
in glaze, the pallid clipper
shipwrecked on the lid.

Marly Youmans

A South Carolina native currently living in upstate New York, MARLY YOUMANS is the author of eight books of fiction and poetry. Her newest book is *The Throne of Psyche*, a collection of poetry from Mercer University Press; *Claire* (Louisiana State University Press, 2005) collects many of her early poems. Her novels are: *Val/Orson* (U.K.: P. S. Publishing, 2009); *The Wolf Pit* (New York: Farrar, Straus and Giroux, 2001, winner of The Michael Shaara Award); *Catherwood* (New York: Farrar, Straus and Giroux, 1996); and *Little Jordan* (Boston: David R. Godine, 1995). *The Curse of the Raven Mocker* (New York: Farrar, Straus and Giroux, 2003) and *Ingledove* (New York: Farrar, Straus and Giroux, 2005) explore American materials for fantasy, fusing the Celtic and Cherokee folkways of the Southern Appalachians. Forthcoming are: a collection of poems, *The Foliate Head* (UK: Stanza Press); a book-length poem, *Thaliad* (Montreal: Phoenicia Publishing); two novels from P. S. Publishing, *Glimmerglass* and *Maze of Blood*; and *A Death at the White Camellia Orphanage*, winner of the inaugural Ferrol Sams Award of Mercer University Press.

THE BOOK OF YSTWYTH

For Clive, to honor his sixtieth birthday retrospective exhibition, The National Library of Wales, Aberystwyth, 2011

The Blue Marches

*'... this early painterly approach to objects can be
seen in Journey's End, the little still-life/landscape
painting of my dad's tea mug standing in front of
Tretower Castle.'* —Clive Hicks-Jenkins

There's nothing here bejeweled with twig and flower,
No wolfish fur that burns as if a kiln
Had been flung wide to let in sprays of salt,
And most of all, no story, wings, or saint.
Instead there is the seepage of a blue
Not twilight: low, continual dim glow
Dispersed from borderlands beyond this world.

So here is landscape as the stillest life,
So here is still life hunkered in the grass,
Estranged from lamplit houses, grown outscale.
There's nothing here but cup and keep and tree,
And tree resembles keep, and keep is tree
Truncated—cup is stump of leaning tree.

No teller yet, unless the tale be one
Older than the famed white book of Rhydderch,
Older than the red of Hergest, older
By far than these . . . Fetch me a magic fruit
So I can taste its glistening cells and gulp
The stubborn words that linger out of reach.

In blueing light, a father's mug might be
The grail, might be Welsh cauldron, wombed with life,
Might over-brim with death-drink, colorless.
There's nothing but a shadow in the cup!
Its clipper ship in sail is doldrum-glazed,
Forgets the fragrance of darjeeling seas.

The motte, a mound of good Welsh earth, was his,
As was the tower vacant to the sky,
The kingdom known as Powys long ago,

And all the rainy borderland of blue—
All things that flee and hide in borderlands
Between the earth and sky belonged to him.

But now he has passed through that realm of dreams
And left you wondering by hills of earth,
And long you'll muse, and long you'll meditate
And never understand the world you brushed
Across that sheet of paper: world where tree
Is keep, and keep is tree, and cup can loom
As high as high Tretower or a tree.

Journey's End, 1999

Hermitry

Sunday when the bells
Were ringing, I dreamed a fine,
High singing in air—

An oval of leaves
Aspired, became cloud. I cried
To the Lord, "Spare me

From maiden-doom, flesh
Conflagrate in marriage-bed,"
And touched the little

Apples of my breasts
And braids that said I was not
Mine, nor Christ's alone.

They never warned me
That God's reply is direful,
Unlike anything.

I slipped into sleep
Within sleep, dreamed the swollen
Womb of an oak tree,

My veins suckling sap . . .
A portal slit allowed light,
Dilated, clasped head

And shoulder: I eased
Like a tender flower-bud
From the lips of tree,

Below a Venus
Mound of leaves—a boy so new
In his second birth,

He scarcely marked day's
Magic cauldron, its wildfire
Breaking in the skies,

The blast of power
Or the exoskeleton
That armed the angel

Whose eyes glanced away,
A delicate intrusion:
The hands offered life

Guised as *bara brith*
That in another instant
The boy took and ate.

The Man Who Lived in a Tree, 2003-4

Master Jug And Lady Candle Stick

The Blue Jug, 2006

With hands on hips and foliate attire,
　　The candlestick is all umbrageousness,
A shady lady who has stripped the trees
　　At upper right to flock her dress with leaves,
A woman apt to give or take offence,
　　Set resolute beside the one-armed jug.
Her wide blue boat of hat upholds a stub
　　With candlewick to warn his waters off—
She'll have no wild outpourings of his love,
　　No boarding of the levees of her skirts.
She doesn't know that he, entrenched in peace,
　　Is musing only of the color blue
And how he can by rounding clasp the sea
　　Until his wheel-turned soul grows chasmal-deep.
Impaled upon a thorn, the little fish
　　At lower right perceives what she cannot
And dreams cloud-cuckoo lands below the waves—
　　Will get there just as soon as Master Jug
Can gather all the seas inside himself,
　　Enspelling blue chimeric revery.

Dear Peregrine,

You said "phantasmagoria" and asked
Just how such things happen, how life changed,
And how I, burning, could embrace a blaze
Like Daniel striding, singing in the threads
Of windblown fire that seemed but harvest wheat,
The summer color of a lion's pelt . . .

My shaping was a strangeness to the world,
Announced by angel messenger: *Hervé*
Would be devoted to the Lord, and two
Predestined as my parents would be matched
And parted in a dream of holiness.
My mother prayed my eyes be undeceived.
My father prayed me visions sent from God.
They made a child the messenger foretold.

I was a little boy immured in night,
A land where Rivanone ran quicksilver
Through shade of trees, my mother Rivanone,
Where *father* meant a voice that shook the boughs
But once had lingered by a throne to sing:
Hyvarnian the bard, who bade me be
Like him; who died too soon. What did I know,
A blind small boy for whom no one looked king?
The world meant inkiness of stones or trees,
The world meant stream that whispered *Rivanone*.

Spiring aloft, a sapling in the woods,
I sang my father's hymns of rue and cheer
And begged for coins to feed his Rivanone.
Then came my frolic, curl-tailed dog that danced
About my feet and chased the leaves with joy
And skimmed his name in barks across the stream.

Some say that forests are best cleansed by coals,
That plants upfling their forms as if renewed
When wildfire passes by—one day a sluice

Of fiery gold fell down from heaven's courts.
I swam inside its waterfall of sun
Until I sensed by second sight the face
That hides itself within a glowing tree.
And then I glimpsed, though dimly, stems and roots
And waves of syllables, as if the monks
Had drawn the world with dark calligraphy
To tell me how all things were made of word
That issued burning from the mouth of God.

The wolf was tangled up with what I knew—
Scathe-mouthed, he rushed to scoop my little dog
And make a tidbit of his dainty shape
Before he slammed between my empty arms.
I somehow knew the wildfire of his fur
Was kindled with the tinder of the words,
And all the world was innocent of guile.
The more he fixed a bracelet of his teeth
Around my arm, the more I sang out love
To rock the earth and unearth rock, to read
The leaf, the stream, the blind fantastic world
Until the forest flashed almighty light.

So now if I should grieve the dark no more,
If I should whoop and carol to the boles,
The wolf my partner in a fearsome dance,
My life phantasmagoria of joy,
Then do not pity me, for I have read
The writing on the walls of eyeless earth
And do not blame the wolf for anything,
For God Almighty, bard above all bards,
Has crowned his head with glory like a saint's
And set the words of wildfire in his fur.

Pax tecum,
Hervé

Furious Embrace, 2007

Catriona's Plate

I. Woman as Delft

Ynysypandy Slate Mill – Toy Theatre with
Delft Plate and Pomegranates, 2004

Up center, down center, and apron, she
Is dominating stage and drops of scenery:
Her flower-painted presence calls the eye
To fly old walls of fieldstone, magically restored,
Fish-skeletons of branches tipped with green,
And pilgrim's scallop shell that crowns proscenium.

Why is her stage-set kingdom painted blue
Like sky or sea? Is she to sail somewhere through cloud
Or ocean? Must she be eternally
Moored at harbor, freighted with ripe pomegranates?

II. Delft as Memento Mori

Delft Plate and Sea Thrift, St. Govan's Head, 2005

Earthly all is dangerous to china—
Blunted seal-brown shapes of cliffs, then plunging absence.
The sea goes dark with something like a thought.
St. Govan's little oratory is unseen,
As secret in the earth as was the bell
That pirates stole and angels thrust inside a stone.

The Delft's as lovely-fragile as before,
But someone's tasted pomegranates snug with seed:
The plate is vacant. Sprigs of sea thrift kiss
The lip in ceding to the wind's invisibles.

CATRIONA URQUHART (1953-2005) was a poet and writer. She produced two books, both illustrated by Clive Hicks-Jenkins – a short story, *Palmyra Jones*, and a sequence of poems, *The Mare's Tale*, conceived to accompany the exhibition of large-scale drawings by Clive at Newport Museum and Art Gallery. *The Mare's Tale* was published in 2001 with new images commissioned specially by The Old Stile Press. In it the poet celebrates the life and marks the death of Trevor Jenkins, who was both her friend and the artist's father. The poems that follow are all taken from that volume. A third collaboration with Clive was to have been Catriona's new translation of the libretto for Stravinsky's *The Soldier's Tale* but the project was unfinished when she died aged 52.

Poem about the Mari Lwyd

Up here above the oaken house
I crouch down with my apple
on the *croglofft* bed.
No sense in supplication for
what cannot be:
a bodily translation;
some magic to defer
what lies ahead,
some way of breaking free.

For already I can hear them
in the lane.
The argy-bargy Punch and Judy show;
the fiddle, laying down a quaint refrain,
insouciant, rustic, artless, winding, slow,
terrifies
by seeming less
while meaning more.

I lean out of the window,
hand on floor,
and rub a half-moon
with my nightshirt cuff.
It's here now.
I can see it rimed with hoar,
bedecked in roses, grosgrain, bells and ruff.

It comes in at a whacking, clattering run.
The Leader whoas it up and tugs its halter
and guides its blinded head, as to an altar,
up to the hollied porch of our front door:

the ghastly, mocking, diabolic Nun;
the sheeted Bride of the Returning Sun.

We stalwart few, we men of Gwent
Are here to sue for ale and rent
And parley due the Mari Lwyd
With one and all this Christmastide!

Men of Cymru, *welcome here!*
Here's oats and caws, here's flowing beer,
Metheglin sweet and Yuletide cheer.
Prosperity this coming year!

But it is never welcome,
not to me.
I would forbid it entry if I could.
I'd lock the door and swallow down the key
and never face again the swirling hood
around that gruesome grin,
that monstrous, spectral head.
I'd swap our Christmas plenty
for a begging bowl.
I'd barter all I have
if I might win.
I'd be good forever
if only God would strike it dead;
but Hetty lifts the latch and lets it in.

Punch is good for a laugh
and Horace plays up for a joke;
Judy whisks round with her brush,
the Leader sits down for a smoke.

While the Mari quarters the room
and chases the girls round the table,
the mummers mumble their play
through mouthfuls of food when they're able.

The fiddle is scraping away,
the room is a cauldron of heat.
Mother sits firm by the fire,
Father is up on his feet

telling tales of the long ago times
when there was never enough.
Punch smacks Judy's behind
and Judy sits down in a huff.

The Mari lets loose with its teeth
and nastily nips all the girls.
Everything spins like a fair
with shriekings and streamers and whirls.

Gaslight shoots up with a flare
then settles again with a hiss.
The Leader springs out of his chair,
gives Judy a mistletoed kiss.

I'm watching it all from the hall,
my pink china pig in my fist.
My stomach knots up in a ball.
I squint through a trembling mist.

The door is flung wide to the wall.
The laughter crescendos and dies.
The Mari stands eighteen hands tall:
'I'm ready to take you', it cries.

This is no maypole frolic of fertility
fandangoed round the mare,
no playground Knock out Ginger
and it runs off home.
I'm rooted by the swivelled, hollow stare.

There's more than horseplay that its sights are on.
The gauntlet's down.
No backing off, no turning round.
Between me and the Mari,
lines are drawn.

It flails towards me,
cumbersome,
and leering in the gloom.
I launch myself against its looming maw:
I'll noose it and I'll hobble it,
I'll spancel it and throttle it.
But Mari has me by its grinning jaw.
In vain I try to prise its teeth apart
and fling away the suffocating sheet.
It shakes me like a rattle,
like a kernel in a nut,
then drops me on the floor beside its feet.

Feet, not hooves
and no ordinary feet
but Dai Morgan's from the Tan House farm.
I stay there beaten, breathless
as they junket out the house,
then I crawl back to the croglofft *to get warm.*

Safe in apple-scented air
I lie in bed
and know the balm
of dreaded things being done.
Know that in the future yet unread
I'll struggle with the Mari in my head,
time and time over.
I could feel pity for this cruel beast,
most strange centaur.

But I will fight and not relent
or let it go.
I'll conquer if I can.

I'll ask a golden bridle of Bellerophon.
I'll tame the horse
and free the whimpering man.

Things happen
when a ring is round the moon.
I watch it now.
And hear a thaw wind
strew the churchyard trees
with melting snow.
The squeaking speech of yew
creaks up the lane
and sounds of opening gates
and raucous pleas rise up again,
till, finally, a faint and tinkling bell
is all I hear of Mari and its crew.

I ponder the night's happenings anew:
they're nothing fearsome,
only working men;

tomorrow on Saint Stephen's Day
they'll blood a horse
and go and hunt a wretched little wren.

The Lie of the Land

I knew the way.
I'd been here every season
on childhood visit to the family home.
My father, revelling in the breadth and spread
of land worked deep and long,
would shoulder me above the whispering corn
as once he'd brought the lambs down
from the farm.

Scorched on the retina's compass,
from this vantage all was conned.
Two farms, left and ahead,
Oak House above, the church beyond.
The mapping points of happiness,
the family bond,
measured by my father's rhythmic tread.

An interim of thirty years or so
has not wrought so much ill upon this land.
Inhabitants of house and farm are gone
and poles with singing wires
march up the hill and make a stand
along a tree-line, taller now,
and broadened out with sapling oak and birch;

yet I am forced to recognise
only that I'm lost
and cannot find the track that wound up
to the stile behind the church.

Unnerved by dislocation, here I sit
with my companions in a field of hay.
Disappointment with what should have been,
with what should rightfully unfurl,
casts its shadow on our sunny day
and gives uncertainty its sway
upon the certain world.

A farmer, whistling up his dog below the brook,
halts to ask us if we've lost our way.
Ignorance is hard to own
in circumstances such as these and so
I stall with desultory chat,
convince myself that nothing is amiss,
I talk of this and that:

give out my antecedents,
stake my claim on shifted ground with casual arm,
then finally, with rueful shrug,
enquire the whereabouts
of churchyard stile and farm.

Once they're pointed out, it's obvious.
How could it be any other way?
The axis of my world tilts back again,
the spinning points of reference remain.
Except for one.

Intruders on the landscape since my time,
yet so discreetly placed you'd think they grew;
as natural as the trees they interlace,
the lines of power poles dotted on the blue,
all stretching out in punctuated mile.

'Your father staked them out in 'sixty-one.
The Board erected them in 'sixty-two.
Just follow up his lines – you'll hit the path.
Follow Trevor's lines – you'll see the stile!'

We mark each pole we pass and climb the hill.
We shoulder, each, another kind of weight.
Astride the stile, I look from where we've come

and sense the power of land to generate,
to interweave with what once was
and what has now become,
to yield:

as gently
and as easily
as field on folded field.

Standing now, I make a survey
of what it was
I thought I knew.
I'm different too, of course,
I'm not as tall.
Necessarily, I take a different view.

Pegasus

You came back in June
full of the wonders of Virginia
and the Blue Ridge.

We tackled the tomatoes:
when and how to feed;
'only when the first truss sets',
and watering;
'don't let them drown';

debated on the merits
of simply lopping off dead roses
as against a careful prune above new eyes;
how early and how late.
Your arguments won out,
experience more telling than a manual's dictate.

In August, you came here every day
to keep your eye on things
while we holidayed away.
Temperatures soared.

Now you are ill, suddenly,
gravely,
in a narrow hospital bed.

You're struggling,
tucked taut as a bud of balsam,
eyes, trusting, innocent as bluebells.

'How did I get this? Where did it come from?'
My chest tightens with the love I bear you
but I only shake my head

and proffer gifts: Fred Hando's *Journeys in Gwent*,
a bunch of bright anemones,
a flask of home-made soup.

You take a mouthful just to please me;
you have no strength to lift a book.
Journeys are inner now, my brave Odysseus,

and you are drowning.
I plunder all mythologies for meaning.
What stalks your strangled senses, tussling the sheet?

Is it the Mari still? Is it careering there?
Or are you now wild Neptune
thrashing down sea horses, trident at your feet?

I pray for Pegasus to wing you clear.

Monitors bleep.
Sonar soundings of the depths you swim in now.
Unfathomable seas.

Sometimes you make a strike for shore
and surface, desperate, panting, glazed;
then sink back crushed

by time's slow snake
and how long it takes
to make a promised place.

All that autumn the plants you'd watered for me
bloomed to bursting;
your pruning and pinching out bore fruit.

Bishop of Llandaff flamed till Christmas;
tomatoes, peppers, filled jars and bowls for weeks;

cuttings took root.

Andrea Selch

The poems of ANDREA SELCH have been
published in *Prairie Schooner*, *Calyx*, *The
MacGuffin*, *Luna*, *The Asheville Poetry Review*
and *Oyster Boy*, among others. Her first
collection of poems, *Succory*, was published
by Carolina Wren Press in 2000, and her
second, *Startling*, by Turning Point Books in
2004. *Boy Returning Water to the Sea: Koans
for Kelly Fearing*, a series of Selch's poems with
images by the late William Kelly Fearing, was
published by the Cockeyed Press in 2009. Selch
joined the board of Carolina Wren in 2001,
and now serves as its president. She lives in
Hillsborough, North Carolina, with her partner
and their two children.

Kevin and the Blackbird's Nest

The nest is tilted, almost spilling
but still the boy does not restore it,
after all, the earth on its axis
is angled, so much in the world's
off-kilter and still surviving.

So much in the world is tilted, spinning,
thinks the boy with the aquiline nose,
so he holds, holds still, for how long
he doesn't know. The blackbird visits,
flitting to and fro. Is it spring or fall?

When will he know it's time
to pick up and go? *Grace à* his steady hand
the fledglings will have flown and finally,
finally—the boy's face grown into a man's—
love will find him, tilting there.

Battle Ground

A battle is dance between warriors; at first
they bow to each other as if no harm will be done,
but their armor is oiled and polished—
it smells of blood—and their rough gloves
softened with sweat; the clashing of swords
makes all of them see white.
                              Even George,
on the night he meets the dragon at Selene,
beholds nothing more than a large winged lizard
whose scales clank like armor and whose breath
could scald the hair from his balls.
He could kill him/her/it and still be inclined
to dance—if he didn't have other fish to fry.
"Come on then, play your next card"
the dying dragon seems to say;
it's a bright day now, in the middle of the night,
and we have all our dragons to slay.
But Georgie Porgie hesitates,
rather to kiss the dragon than make it die.

The prophet disturbed

A sharp stone in hand, like any good son of god,
I try and write them, the images—creatures,
angels, acts—that bubble behind my lids
before I fall asleep in the sun.
                              I'm nearly
blinded, not from the sun or clouds
(though clouds do have a way of blinding)
but by the crowd carrying along their
Slapper! Slattern! Whore!
                              Who among them
has not given her a coin, drunk of her joy?
Who among us has not adored folly?
Looking down, they shift from foot to foot,
their muttering hushed.
                              Then, as they retire, I
see their sandals have erased my lovely writing.
What's left—mute ground and myself, roused.

The Ghost of an Ox Visits the Broken Yoke

In the absence of memory, the wooden thing,
splintering, is mere curiosity. Nonetheless
the ox, his strong back relaxed, feels drawn
to it, returns daily to sit by it, thinking.
"Git up, gee! Gee!" the ox seems to hear it say,
and he's almost nudged from contentment.

In the distance, like large snowflakes
on the mountain peak, sheep graze mechanically,
growing their coats.

Matins at Penparc Cottage

Though he tries to tamp them down,
his memories come through his dreams
and memories of dreams, how many years
he hunted glory, clanging about the countryside
on his father's horse, or worse, in cities:
what wasn't stage for his dilation was his green room,
all his own. The moment's past where
he could (and did) strip off all the raiment
that suddenly was not his own, orphaning himself,
naked as the day he was born. Funny—he
didn't feel at all forsaken, not the least bit,
just a little cold. Now, he's that a thousand-fold,
and also old.

But, before his begging bowl is filled,
the morning prayers must still be sung,
and Francis in his ragged tunic stands
above the garden and says Our Father
where the sparrows and the long-tailed tits,
the bullfinches and chaffinches
flit among dahlias in their bishops' caps,
bellflowers and the late-blooming toad lilies.

The birds, despite their finery, are always poor
and do not dream—even of harmony, mild spring wind.

The Blind Boy and His Wolf

Blood is the texture of the meeting of wolf and dog.

And after the growls and yelps died away
I felt it flaking from the wolf's pelt
as he leaned into me in greeting,
Enough boy, enough.

Like a wave he rolled in, swallowed my dog.

Blind since birth, I cannot picture him
Cadmium, Madder and Black, with a slanted Siberian eye,
but ask why should he stay with me? Why?

Blood is the texture of the meeting of wolf and dog,
and to destroy, the wolf's ploy.

And now, with a wolf for eyes,
tout-le-monde seems prey
and runs from us
though he is tame
and I, Hervé.

Dave Bonta

A poet and editor, DAVE BONTA is from the eastern edge of western Pennsylvania. He is a founder and co-editor of *Qarrtsiluni*, an online literary magazine, and has been publishing his own material on the web since 2003, mostly at his blog *Via Negativa*. Some of his poems are collected at *Shadow Cabinet*, a self-published e-book, and he keeps a daily journal of prose-micropoems at *The Morning Porch*. His collection of poems, *Odes to Tools*, was published by Phoenicia Publishing, Montreal, in 2010. The poems that follow were written in response to the eight paintings in the series The Temptations of Solitude.

The Grave Dug by Beasts

Solitude is a burrow
into which you fold yourself
like a letter into an envelope

stamped Return to Sender.
It's the metal flag raised
for the postman

or for the prisoner of conscience
still loyal to his cause,
waiting for the sky to change

its mind about being a roof.
His letters come back to him
with all the words blacked out,

leaving only the punctuation:
tooth marks, claw marks, tails.
This is the solitude

of St. Anthony, beset by lust
& anger, indolence & madness:
who wouldn't want

to lose himself in
an unmarked grave
excavated by indifferent beasts?

The Comfort of Angels
Attending the Dying

You always dreamed of a death
in the open, stopping at the wye
in the highway that runs past
the shell of the old mill,
the land like a black lung
infiltrated by bronchial trees.
You'd keep your eyes pinched shut
against whatever brightness might spoil
the immaculate desolation.
After so many tiresome years
of living for others, this would be
your own time at last,
alone on the baked earth.

But it seems the Father won't let you go
so easy, sends a pair of his goons
to bookend your shoulders
& breathe cabbage in your ears.
Meaty arms wrap around your chest
like pythons & begin to squeeze.
Let's go for a ride, they whisper.
Death in the open—you're finding out—
means all bets are off. The air turns
dangerous with blades.

The Man Who Lived in a Tree

Turn up the lights on the hominid pen.
It's feeding time, though some
don't even know they're hungry.
You can give them each
a slice of manna if you like.

See the one who squats in the crotch
of that tree? Almost since birth
he's exiled himself from the ground.
Unlike the others, he seems to realize
something here is missing—
a grotesque sensitivity that makes him
a wolf in this wood, this tree
he clings to like a mother.
When the wind agitates its leaves
he hugs himself & rocks
back & forth, moaning.

Unlike the others who gibber with awe,
he wants nothing to do with us,
& recoils from your face
as if from a stone that the river
never learned how to read.
But see how his tree glows
in this lurid light, like a harp
rearing above a dark-suited orchestra?
Someday soon we will reunite it
with its former companions,
that whole forest enjoying
eternal life: value-added products
of our loving care.

The Penitent Roasted by the Sun

For the sin of thirst, surround yourself with mirrors
& wait for baptism.

For the sin of sensitivity, plant yourself among lawn ornaments,
neon-bright & obvious.

For the sin of poverty, expose yourself
to the cauterizing desert of the sky.

Build a stockade between the storm door & the doghouse
to incarcerate the green thieves of light.

You have lived too many years as a parasite,
drunk the high-fructose corn syrup of paradise.

It's time to tunnel into the brazen day
& shrug off your integument, oh locust.

Under what basket or milk crate have
you hidden your cry?

The Barbarian Brought Down by a Lioness

Did he taste of loneliness, sour & marmoreal,
that man from away who came out here
to get away from himself?

What vapors rose from the punctured
balloon of his gut, which he used to tap
with the small end of a fist when explaining

the pull of mountain scenery,
the open spaces & abundant peace?
He would settle here

as lightly as a leaf, he swore, praying
for the developers to be enveloped
& the subdividers subjected to division.

They didn't feel the wilderness
the way he did, living off the land,
conscious only of God's grace

as he looked back: the poor earth raw
from harrow & bulldozer, a snaggletoothed jumble
of lighthouse, smokestack, steeple.

Nothing like the orderly ridges rippling
under his attacker's pelt—that figment
of the blue distance suddenly at hand.

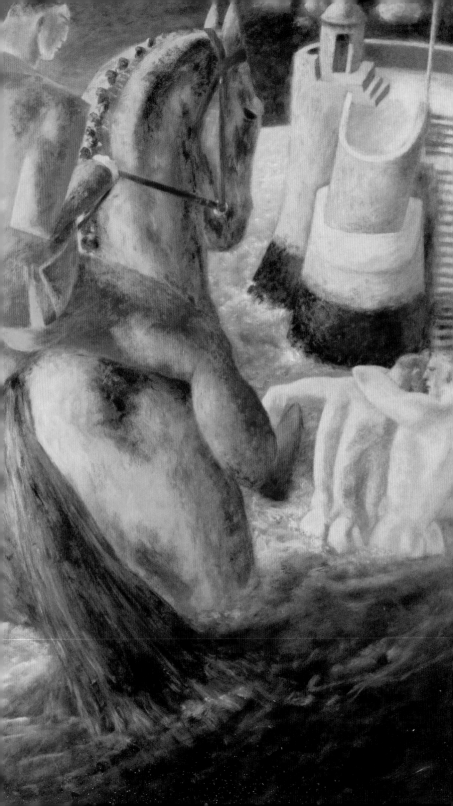

The Celibate Couple Pursued

Who let these two pawns crowd
into a single square? The game
requires that we each defend
our solitude. We have banished
the bird from the tree & the tree
from the horizon. But now

the white knight wrestles
with temptation: can't he take
the direct route to head them off,
pin them against the straight-
arrow castle, instead of sidling up
in waltz steps like some kind
of goddamned dandy?

The black & white squares begin
to merge—a gray quicksand.
His horse grows scaley,
anadromous, gathers itself
for a leap worthy of Cúchulainn.

The disobedient pair flee
to the far edge of their flat earth
& turn into queens,
resplendent & terrifying.
The watchman bawls
from his tall tower,
Check & Check & Mate.

The Righteous Man Surprised by the Devil

Chopping wood & carrying water
at the old collieries,
a sudden smug thought popped up:
*I should be enlightened
in no time!* And just like that,
no-time snagged me

there in front of the tipple,
by the monkey puzzle tree.
The ground buckled as if
from a blast of dynamite.
My ears filled with roaring
from the long-closed pit.

Pride is an itch you can only
ignore for so long until
Old Scratch surfaces again,
lurid & ridiculous, like
a malevolent penis with two
blind eyes instead of one.

I dropped to my knees,
sank into the vetch & nettles
while the others went on
with their meditations,
lowering buckets into the well
of the long afternoon.

Only a dog paused to watch
my clawing at the air.
A rash spread above that un-
reclaimed stripmine like the glow
from some legendary sunset
in a land without smog.

The Beating of the Falsely Accused

This ash-colored immigrant come
to steal an honest man's job—
give him the business, why don't you.
Let every slack muscle learn

what real work feels like,
how it aches & bruises.
Then let him go fishing
with a cast-iron kettle around his neck.

The sanitarium should've known better,
trying to hire orderlies from outside.
We're hungry here.
The sun itself only gets in

a few licks each day,
& the sea eats like a drunk—
a nibble here & a nibble there
to steady itself against the shore.

We've all been tenderized.
We marinate in the tall salt cellars
the rapeseed oil cans
the cold ovens of our houses,

watch the flickering pilot light
in the corner of the room
& dream of an all-you-can-eat buffet.
Let us pray for the firm

flesh of angels, white,
with eyes that can sprout,
that can finger, that can shove
green fists through the dirt.

Callum James

As a writer, CALLUM JAMES' interests and themes have tended towards the darker side of eroticism, urban life, familial relationships and spirituality. He lives in Portsmouth from where he can wave to his childhood home across the Solent on the Isle of Wight. He earns money dealing in secondhand books, vintage photos and anything else made of paper and by publishing small limited editions of the work of queer Victorians and Edwardians. His blog is *callumjames.blogspot.com*.

Stations of the Cross

I. Jesus is condemned to death

Man and man
are standing in the
white stone and high
columns of palaces.

Silence and frustration
hanging as the dust in
warm air circulates.

Questions about truth
are soft curls of
sunlight and silence,

and somewhere in the years
beyond this room and this judgement,

a million voices speak

with him

of injustice

in a blinding white silence.

II. Jesus is given his cross

Skin
and splinter
and blood.

Cracked grain and tight knot
to be worked and eased
like a muscle strung in pain

and butting against rough wood.
Rough hewn it will weigh down
a line of vertebrae

and twist through years
into precious metals, mother of pearl, soft
engraving and small pendant.

Dead wood will flower
and flow like the water
drawn on its grain.

Skin
and splinter
and blood.

VII. Jesus falls for the second time

Is it the world tips
or the pitch of liquid
in a dizzied ear?

The sickening spin
and the sudden
unavailability
of grip
conspire.

There must be tears
down here where the view
is sandal-straps
and calloused toes
and dog's paws and
tall, tall people
who rise above and seem complete.

God has crumpled
to a bag of stick limbs
and is empty as dust.

There must be tears down here.

This is a fall
that will shake the world.

IX. Jesus falls for the third time

Down and down
to where toenails
are hard yellow
and breath is an intake of dirt
and where the gutters
run damp and stinking at noon.

Where the sun has gone:
an eclipse of legs and hem
lines.

Even the fascinated wince,
even their intake of breath
stutters as body and bloodied
wood crack heavy to the grit.

Light twists and heaven is,
for only a moment, dark.

And the moment stretches
and it will always be there
in the memory of angels.

XIII. Jesus is taken down from the cross

Hard to hold for lightness,
floating to the ground in the
care of arms; guided like a feather

to rest:

the body.

Free from all weight, finally,
laid like a soft rag on the ground
here is the final proof

of God:

a body.

The Boy and The Wolf

I. Hervé is born

Born in November
in the short days:
born leaning against
the slanting rain:
born from a frozen prayer
to a bleak God.
Knitted in solitude
in a womb
pricked by a vow and
surprised into swelling.

II. Hervé's first sight

Pushing aside dark earth,
a milk-film
over his eyes:
this small stone of a boy
ate dirt, while the
glory danced white
on blank, black retinas.

III. Hervé learns about the world

Grasses by their hissing
and sharp cuts:
fur by its musk
and static crackle:
snowdrops by their tinkling
on his fingertips;
the world attacked him,
was a lightning strike
inside his chest.

IV. Hervé has visions

And in his twilight
a light more sumptuous
seeped in;
a bending tree and he
was fighting dragons,
the broken sun on
rough-topped rivers
and he was rich in diamonds,
smiling mad.
He fell to pray
before the hilltop shepherd
who flexed an angel's wings:
a cloak that rippled
threadbare in the wind.

V. Hervé sees The Wolf

He saw,
the day The Wolf came,
he saw the threat
and the salvation.
He saw the shape of undergrowth:
thicket-dark, triangular,
he saw a head
the shape of a snarl
in heated breath.

VI. Hervé's dog is killed by The Wolf

What did he see
in the smell of hot-iron
from the slaughtered dog?
What bright colours,
what beauty was in his hands
slipping through
spilled intestines?
What overwhelming, pungent
touch of heaven came?

VII. The Wolf attacks Hervé

And The Wolf turned
with the world
around the boy
and teeth the temperature
of ice pushed through skin:
here where the heavy pelt,
muscle-packed, pressed
the boy and his skin tore
breaking the line of holiness
that runs around a saint.

VIII. Hervé redeems The Wolf

A blinding alleluia of light
as from the boy
love tumbled,
burst like river-diamonds,
mingling with The
Wolf's breath,
flooding the grasses, fur,
the snowdrops,
heating the prayer
that made him.

IX. Hervé and The Wolf together

That moment hung,
a stopped raindrop,
a never falling leaf
within his soul: quivering.
It abided there.
The Wolf abided
at the centre of him.

X. Hervé prays

Unable to contain it
all inside, the boy
began to howl;
a voice of red and gold,
a passion, sung like petals
spewing, uncontrollable
from God's own lips,
and everything that heard him
leaned and swayed
and healed a little
as he lay his head
forever
on the shoulder of The Wolf.